Coming Soon...

TORNADOES CAN MAKE IT
RAIN CRABS
WEIRD FACTS ABOUT NATURAL DISASTERS

FLIES TASTE
WITH THEIR FEET!

WEIRD FACTS ABOUT INSECTS

A WEIRD-BUT-TRUE BOOK

by
Melvin & Gilda Berger
illustrated by Robert Roper

SCHOLASTIC INC.
New York Toronto London Auckland Sydney

ISBN 0-590-93994-7

Text copyright © 1997 by The Gilda Berger Revocable Trust.
Illustrations copyright © 1997 by Robert Roper.
All rights reserved. Published by Scholastic Inc.

12 11 10 9 8 7 6 5 4   8 9/9 0 2/0

Printed in the U.S.A.   40

First Scholastic printing, January 1997

INSECTS ARE AMAZING

FLIES TASTE WITH THEIR FEET

Flies have six feet. They use them to walk, of course. But they also use them for tasting! First they step on the food. If it tastes good — they sip it up!

Honeybees, butterflies, and moths also taste with their feet. They like certain plants. When they land on a flower, their feet tell them if it's fit to eat.

Many female butterflies only lay eggs on certain plant leaves. So they walk on the leaf. If it passes the taste test they stop right there.

? **DID YOU KNOW?**

- Most insects can pick out four tastes: sweet, sour, salty, and bitter. These are the same basic tastes you get with your tongue.

MOSQUITOES SMELL WITH THEIR FEELERS

Mosquitoes don't have noses. Instead they have two long feelers on their heads called antennae. Antennae can sniff out food, danger, and other mosquitoes.

Almost all insects have antennae. But the best smeller of all is the male *emperor moth*. This insect can pick up the odor of a female moth from seven miles away!

DID YOU KNOW?

- **Almost all insects use their two antennae for smelling. But some insects also use them to feel, taste, and hear.**

GRASSHOPPERS BREATHE THROUGH THEIR SIDES

Grasshoppers and most other insects breathe air just like humans. But insects don't have noses or lungs. They breathe through tiny holes along the sides of their bodies! Do you suppose insects have runny sides when they catch cold?

DID YOU KNOW?

- Each breathing hole leads to a large tube that divides into smaller and smaller tubes. These tubes bring air to all parts of the insect's body.

ANTS CAN LIVE WITHOUT HEADS

A scientist once cut the head off an ant. The rest of the ant walked around for over a month!

Every insect has a main brain in its head and mini-brains in other parts of the body. It needs the head and main brain to eat. But the mini-brains let the insect walk, fly, and lay eggs — until it starves to death.

DID YOU KNOW?

- A few kinds of insects, such as dragonflies and honeybees, are probably deaf.

CRICKETS HEAR WITH THEIR KNEES

Look for a *cricket's* ears. But you'll not find them! So how do crickets hear?

Crickets (and *katydids*, too) hear with flat spots near the knees on their front legs! The flat spots work just like your eardrums. They pick up sound waves and send the messages to the brain.

But not all flat spots are in the same place on insects' bodies. Locusts, moths, and grasshoppers have "ears" on their sides. And butterflies hear with flat spots near the base of their wings.

Many other insects hear with tiny body hairs. Mosquitoes and ants have hairy antennae. Caterpillars are hairy everywhere!

DRAGONFLIES GET THE PICTURE

Dragonflies are like most insects. They have two huge eyes. But each eye has many separate lenses. In fact, the dragonfly has more lenses than any other insect. Would you believe 30,000 in each eye?

All together the lenses let the insect see front, back, and to the sides! Remember that the next time you try to catch a dragonfly!

DID YOU KNOW?

- **Almost all insects can see clearly for about one yard. Anything beyond that looks blurry.**

LAUGH LINES

Did you hear about the eye doctor who went crazy trying to fit a dragonfly with glasses?

STAGGERING STATISTICS

- For every person on earth there are one million insects!

- Insects are four times as numerous as all other animals *combined*!

- One square mile of rural land has more insects than there are humans in the whole world!

MIGHTY MIDGETS

Insects are much stronger than humans — for their size! An ant can lift a crumb 50 times as heavy as itself. If you were as strong, you could carry a ton of bricks.

A *flea* can jump about 13 inches. If you could do that you'd be able to jump the length of two football fields!

Cockroaches can run about 2 $\frac{1}{2}$ miles an hour. At that rate, you could race along at 130 miles an hour!

GREAT DISGUISERS

Insects are small in size, with lots of enemies. Luckily many have good camouflage and are often hard to find.

Ithomiid and *pierid butterflies* have see-through wings. When resting on plants, these bugs are almost invisible!

Katydids and many *long-horned grasshoppers* look like green leaves. *Prominent moth caterpillars* and *leaf butterflies* resemble dead plant parts.

Walking sticks and *geometrid moth caterpillars* are mistaken for dry twigs.

Mantids, *stink bugs*, and geometrid moths blend into tree bark.

LAUGH LINES

Have you seen any good-looking insects?

No, they're all "bugly"!

FOR THE RECORD

Fastest flyer: Dragonflies have been clocked at over 30 miles an hour!

Fastest wings: At over 60,000 beats a minute, the *biting midge*, or *no-see-um*, holds the record!

Slowest wings: The *swallowtail butterfly* drifts along at a lazy 300 wing beats a minute!

Loudest: People can hear the noisy male *cicada* from about a mile away!

Heaviest: The *goliath beetle* of Africa tips the scale at a quarter pound!

Longest: The *giant stick insect* sometimes reaches one foot in length!

Smallest: The *fairy fly* is only $1/100$ inch long. It's small enough to pass through the eye of a needle.

Longest life: Some *queen termites* live to be 50 years old!

Shortest life: Most *mayflies* live less than one day!

FLIES, FLEAS
& MOSQUITOES

LIQUIDS ONLY

Flies often land on bread, cake, or fruit. But they can only sip liquids, not eat solid food. So what's a fly to do?

Before eating, the fly spits on the food. This turns it into a liquid. Then the fly lowers its spongelike mouth, and soaks it up!

TRICKY FEET

Imagine walking on walls, hanging from ceilings, even climbing up mirrors and windows! For houseflies, it's simple!

A sticky liquid comes out of the hollow hairs on their feet. The tacky liquid holds them in place. Yet it lets them lift their feet to move forward.

EYE TO EYE

What's weird about the *stalk-eyed fly*? Its eyes are at the end of long, thin stems! The distance from eye to eye is greater than from head to tail!

Stalk-eyed flies sometimes fight other stalk-eyed flies. They stand head to head and match stalk lengths! The insect with the longer stalks wins the battle — without bloodshed!

SHARP NOSED

The *tsetse fly* often lands on animals or humans. Down goes its head with the long, pointy beak. The sharp tip cuts right through anything — from rhinoceros skin to a heavy jacket! The beak passes into the victim's body, and the fly sips the victim's blood!

DID YOU KNOW?

- Tsetse flies sometimes carry dangerous germs. These germs can cause sleeping sickness in humans. Up to 20,000 people a year die of sleeping sickness disease.

FOOD FOR THOUGHT

Some insects never gain weight. One flea in a lab lived for nearly six years without eating! *Mayflies* and *nonbiting midges* do not eat at all.

DID YOU KNOW?

- Caterpillars can only live a few hours without eating.

FLYING MACHINE

Flies usually fly forward. But a few kinds — *hoverflies, bee flies, flower flies,* and *dragonflies* — can fly forward and backward. These flies can even hover like helicopters!

DID YOU KNOW?

- Flies have only one (not two) pair of wings. Before takeoff, they do not run or jump. They just beat their wings and away they go.

FOR THE RECORD

Smallest: The biting midge is only $\frac{1}{20}$ inch long!

Biggest: The *mydas fly* of South America measures 3 inches from head to tail and 3 inches from wingtip to wingtip!

Speediest: Houseflies zip through the air at about $4\frac{1}{2}$ miles an hour — or more if trying to escape a fly swatter!

Longest Time Flying: One *drosophila fly* flew for $6\frac{1}{2}$ hours without stopping!

ROTTEN KID

The young *gall midge* grows from an egg inside its mother's body. For food it eats its mother's insides! When fully grown, it leaves the mother — a dead, empty shell!

DID YOU KNOW?

- The *African midge* doesn't mind the cold. One was kept at 452 degrees below zero — and lived!

FAIR AND SQUARE

Newly hatched *horseflies* are small and look like worms. They are called maggots. The maggots often hide in the sides of ponds and feed on tiny toad tadpoles.

In time, the maggots grow into adult horseflies. The tadpoles grow into adult toads. What happens next? The adult toads play turnabout. They feed on grown-up horseflies!

LAUGH LINES

CUSTOMER: Waiter, what's the fly doing in my soup?

WAITER: It looks like the backstroke!

USEFUL BITES

The *blowfly* can pick up the smell of a dead creature in seconds — even from very far away. The insect flies to the animal and lays eggs on its body. Hours later the eggs hatch into maggots that nibble away at the flesh.

For a long time, doctors thought blowfly maggots in an open wound were dangerous. Then they found that maggots give off a chemical that helps wounds to heal. Today chemists make this helpful drug in their labs.

DID YOU KNOW?

- **Experts use the blowfly's eggs and maggots to decide the time of death of animals — or humans. The results have been used as evidence in court cases.**

INSIDE JOBS

The maggots of the *bot fly* invade a victim's body in crazy ways. One kind of bot fly lays eggs in a horse's jaws or lips. The eggs hatch into maggots that crawl into the animal through its mouth!

Another kind of bot fly lays its eggs on the legs or backs of cattle. The maggots hatch and bore their way through the animal's skin! Once inside, they eat and grow there. They even make breathing holes in the animal's skin! After a year or so, the maggots crawl out, become flies, and flit away.

BURIED IN BUGS

Greenflies, or *aphids*, produce their young very fast. A single aphid can give rise to 50 offspring in just one week! Most get eaten by spiders and ladybugs. But what if all the aphids born in one year survived? They would form a layer nearly 100 miles high over the entire earth!

DID YOU KNOW?

- Many wingless aphids spend their whole life on the same plant on which they were born.

PRIZE JOCKS

Fleas can jump 100 times their height and pull 50 times their weight! Not bad for creatures that measure less than $\frac{1}{8}$ inch in length!

LAUGH LINES

CIRCUS OWNER: I see jumping fleas in my sleep.

DOCTOR: Don't worry, it's a hoptical illusion!

TROUBLESOME FLEAS

Rat fleas are small and ordinary-looking. Yet these little insects are cold-blooded killers! About 600 years ago they took the lives of some 40 million Europeans!

Rat fleas live on black rats and suck their blood for food. As the flea drinks the blood, it picks up deadly germs. When a flea bites a person, the germs pass into the victim's blood. The person falls ill with bubonic plague. Death usually follows within a week.

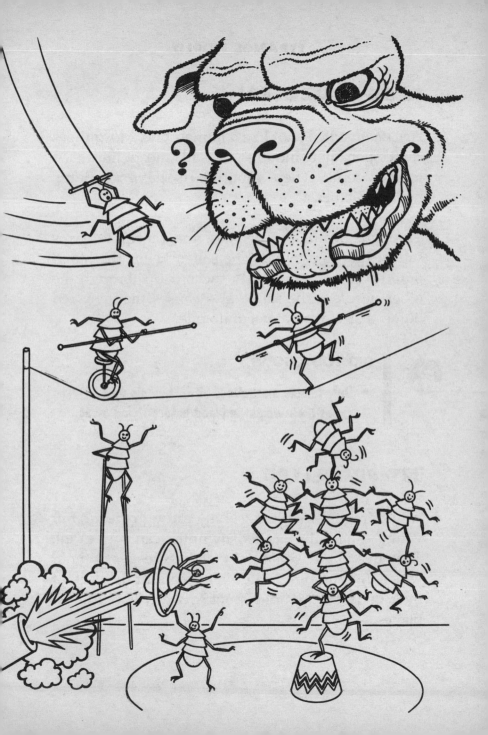

GREAT GUZZLERS

A *mosquito* bite is not like a human bite. Mosquitoes can't open their mouths! Instead, mosquitoes stab their victims. Their mouthparts have six long, hollow needles!

Through one of the needles, the mosquito drips saliva into the wound. The saliva keeps the blood liquid while the mosquito sucks it up through the other needles. The saliva also causes the itchy red bump that we call a mosquito bite.

DID YOU KNOW?

- Only female mosquitoes bite. They sip up to $1\frac{1}{2}$ times their weight in blood before flying away.

JET-PROPELLED

Adult dragonflies flit gracefully through the air. But young dragonflies, called nymphs, can't fly at all. They live in the water and look like beetles without wings. By pumping water in and out of the back of their body the nymphs scoot forward like little jet planes.

DID YOU KNOW?

- A dragonfly nymph eats more than 3,000 insects before becoming an adult.

COLOSSAL FOSSIL

Miners found the fossil of a 310-million-year-old dragonfly. That's not too weird. Except that this dragonfly had a wingspan of over 27 inches! Compare that with the 2-inch wingspan of today's dragonflies.

BUTTERFLIES
AND MOTHS

LICKETY-SPLIT

Butterflies resting on rocks often look like they're eating the rocks! But the insects are *licking*, not eating. They do this to get salt from the stones.

LAUGH LINES

CUSTOMER: Waiter, there's a fly in the butter.

WAITER: Of course, it's a butterfly!

DISGUSTING DISGUISE

The *swallowtail butterfly caterpillar* looks like a yucky bird dropping! Few animals want to go near it. What a great disguise!

?

DID YOU KNOW?

- **Most butterfly caterpillars are either green or brown. Many have spikes, hairs, or bumps that make them hard to swallow.**

TRICK OF THE TRADE

Flashy colors usually mean that an insect is poisonous or bad-tasting. Other animals learn to stay away. Like the *monarch butterfly* with its bright orange wings. Enemies know it tastes dreadful. They leave it alone.

The *viceroy butterfly* is not poisononous or bad-tasting. But it looks like the monarch. So most animals keep their distance!

DO NOT TOUCH

The *saddleback moth* caterpillar is a pretty shade of green with a brown "saddle" in the middle. But beware! Its hairs are poisonous. Touch the caterpillar and you get a rash and high fever!

LONG DISTANCE TRAVELERS

Every fall, millions of monarch butterflies head south from the northern United States and Canada. Many fly more than 2,000 miles to Mexico! But few of them come back. Females lay eggs on the return trip. The adults die — and the offspring come home alone!

FLY-BY BUTTERFLY

You may think the female *marbled white butterfly* is zany. To lay her eggs, she flies over a grassy field, and just drops them! The eggs stick to blades of grass. When the caterpillars hatch, their food is ready and waiting!

RED RAINDROPS

As a butterfly emerges from a chrysalis, or cocoon, it squirts a waste fluid from its body. *Painted lady butterflies* — among others — give off a red fluid! If lots of butterflies come out at once, it seems to be raining blood!

DID YOU KNOW?

- Insect blood is usually colorless, pale green, or straw-colored. The blood fills all the empty spaces in the insect's body.

KEEPING WARM

The *Arctic clouded yellow butterfly* lives where the temperature is often far below zero. To keep from freezing, the clouded yellow warms its wings in the sun. A special liquid in its blood is like a car's antifreeze. It keeps the blood from freezing.

DID YOU KNOW?

- Butterflies cannot fly if their body temperature falls below 86° F.

KEEPING CLEAN

The hairy front legs of the *brush-footed butterfly* are of little help in walking. But they are very useful. The butterfly uses its legs to brush bits of dirt off of its eyes!

CLOGGED EARS

A *moth's* antennae sometimes get jammed with plant pollen. Then the moth cannot hear very well. What can it do? Simply reach up with its legs and clean, clean, clean!

DID YOU KNOW?

- Adult moths do not make holes in woolen clothes. Only moth caterpillars do.

BLOODTHIRSTY MOTHS

The *Malaysian moth* does not eat flower nectar like most other moths. It feeds on blood! Its usual victims are buffalo and other large animals. Thirsty moths will suck blood for up to an hour!

LAUGH LINES

Why didn't the butterfly go to the dance?

Because it was a mothball!

SILKY SURPRISES

The *silk moth* caterpillar is called a silkworm. Its cocoon is made of a single silk thread over a half mile long!

The wild *American silkworm* increases its weight 4,000 times before becoming an adult moth! The *polyphemous moth caterpillar* has an even bigger appetite. It multiplies its weight 80,000 times in just two days!

FOR THE RECORD

Biggest butterfly: *Queen Alexandra's birdwing* has a 12-inch wingspan!

Smallest butterfly: The *western pigmy blue* measures $1/4$ inch from wingtip to wingtip!

Biggest moth: The wingspread of Australia's *Hercules moth* is 14 inches.

Smallest moth: Some *leafminer* moths are only $1/8$ inch across.

BEES, WASPS, ANTS & TERMITES

POWER BEE

A *bumblebee* once pulled a small model car that was about 300 times its own weight. If you had the strength of a bee, you could pull a 10-ton truck!

DID YOU KNOW?

- **Most bees sting once and die. Not the bumblebee. It can sting over and over again.**

HOT AND COLD BEES

Honeybees cool and heat their hives. In summer, some bees fly to the hive entrance and flap their wings. This draws out the hot air and blows in colder air. In winter, the bees gather into a large ball. Then they shake and shiver to raise their temperature. That's togetherness!

NO MERCY

Killer bees sting for almost any reason at all. Running away won't help. The bees can fly faster than you can run. And the bees can chase you for up to a mile!

Sometimes hundreds of killer bees land on the victim. Their stingers slice through clothing and skin. The tips pump poison — about four times as powerful as cobra poison — deep into the flesh!

?

DID YOU KNOW?

- **Killer bees have the same yellow stripes as ordinary honeybees. But they are a little smaller and weigh a bit less.**

GRABBY AND GREEDY

Parasitic wasps lay dozens of eggs inside living caterpillars! When the eggs hatch, the young wasps nibble the flesh of the caterpillar. Later the adult wasps burst out through the caterpillar's side.

HOOKED UP

Many ants sting. But *fire ants* are the worst. They sting and sting and sting!

The fire ant locks its jaws on the victim's skin. Then it lowers its back end and stings. Still holding with its jaws, the ant circles around with its rear end — and stings again! Over and over, the ant wiggles-stings, wiggles-stings, wiggles-stings. When it finally stops, the victim has a small circle of hot, bright-red, painful wounds!

DID YOU KNOW?

- **Fire ants sting about 5 million Americans a year. Almost a million of the victims need medical treatment. About a dozen die of their wounds.**

STORE KEEPERS

Harvester ants collect seeds and chew them into a pulp called "ant bread." They store the bread in their nests and eat it when food is scarce.

HONEY SUCKERS

Honey ants capture tiny insects called *aphids* for a very good reason. Aphids suck juices from plants and produce a liquid called "honeydew." In the ant nest, the honey ants stroke the aphids with their antennae. Each aphid produces a drop of honeydew, which the ants lap up.

Certain honey ants sip so much flower nectar that they grow as big as marbles! These honey storehouses waddle into the nest and dangle by their legs from the roof. From time to time they spit up food for hungry ants to eat!

FORCED LABOR

Amazon ants catch other kinds of ants and make them into slaves! The captured ants feed the Amazon ants and dig their nests. They also care for the eggs and the young. Why do the Amazon ants need all this help? Because their long, curved jaws stop them from helping themselves to food!

DID YOU KNOW?

- Some Amazon ants live in flood areas near the Amazon river. Instead of building nests in the ground, these ants build nests up in the trees.

ARMED ATTACK

Army ants travel in huge groups — from 10,000 to several million. The advancing hordes give off a smell like rotten meat! And their footsteps make a loud, frightening, hissing noise.

No one is safe from marching army ants. They attack even the biggest animals. Hundreds of ants swarm over every victim. They open wide their razor-sharp jaws — and *ZAP!* — slam them shut on the flesh. The ants hang on as they pull and tear at the animal. Sooner or later the creature dies of its wounds.

DID YOU KNOW?

- Army ants are brown and yellow instead of black or brown like ordinary ants. They are also bigger in size.

FOR THE RECORD

Biggest: The *ponerine ants* of the tropics sometimes grow to be over one inch in length!

Smallest: *Pharaoh ants* are as tiny as apple seeds!

EGG-LAYING MACHINES

Termites live in large groups, just like ants. The ruler of the group is the queen termite. She is over 100 times the size of the male termite with whom she mates, and more than 2,000 times as big as the worker termites in the nest.

When stuffed full of eggs, the queen termite looks like a hot dog with a tiny head at the end! Because she is so heavy, she can't walk. She just sits and lays eggs — about one every 3 seconds. That comes to 30,000 a day! Over her lifetime, she can lay 100 million eggs!

DID YOU KNOW?

- **A termite nest may hold a swarm of 5 million termites — all hatched from the eggs of one queen!**

LAUGH LINES

What did one termite say to another in the nest?

It's "swarm" here!

BRILLIANT BUILDERS

Africa's *fungus growing termites* build the biggest insect nests in the world. The record is nearly 42 feet high! Built-in chimneys keep the large mud nests nice and cool.

Jungle termites make their homes in tropical rain forests. It rains here almost every day. These termite nests have umbrellalike tops! Let it rain. The nests stay good and dry.

DID YOU KNOW?

• Termites look like ants but have thicker waists.

LAUGH LINES

Why did the termite run around in circles?

It was trying to make ends meet!

BEETLES, CRICKETS & GRASSHOPPERS

BLOODY BATTLES

The *bloody-nosed beetle* defends itself in a goofy way. When afraid, it squirts red blood from the tip of its snout. And that's before a single punch is thrown!

The *ladybug* squirts blood, too. But its blood is yellow, not red, and awfully smelly! Even goofier — the blood shoots out from its knees!

DID YOU KNOW?

- Sometimes the ladybug is called ladybird or lady beetle. Long ago people believed that eating a ladybug could cure the measles and other diseases.

LAUGH LINES

CUSTOMER: Waiter, there's a ladybug in my soup.

WAITER: Don't worry, it won't drink much!

CHEMICAL WARFARE

Stay away from *bombardier beetles*! When attacked, they tuck their rear end under the body and spew out a foul-smelling, boiling-hot poison.

Darkling beetles spray poison at their worst enemy, the grasshopper mouse. But the mouse knows how to handle it. It grabs the beetle and shoves its rear end into the ground! Now the darkling can't fire. That gives the mouse plenty of time to eat the insect.

DUNG BALLS

Dung beetles live near large grazing animals. The beetles form the animal dung into a ball, which they roll and bury. A female beetle then lays eggs on the buried ball. When the young beetles or grubs hatch, they feed on the dung.

DID YOU KNOW?

- Ancient Egyptians believed dung beetles were sacred creatures. They called them scarabs. Egyptians wore scarab carvings for good luck.

UNDERCOVER

Female *jewel beetles* lay their eggs under the bark of living trees. The eggs hatch into grubs. The wormlike grubs may live in the tree for a very long time.

A few years ago, someone found a live jewel beetle grub in the wooden floor of a church. The church was about 50 years old! Imagine being buried alive for half a century!

WACKY LOVE SONG

The male *deathwatch beetle* attracts a female in a wacky way. He knocks his head against the wooden beams of the old building in which the female lives! She answers by banging with her head.

In olden days, when people heard the knocking sounds they thought it meant that someone in the house was going to die. And that's how the deathwatch beetle got its name!

BIZARRE BUGS

Whirligigs are weird little beetles that live in ponds and quiet streams. They take their name from the way they dart around in circles on top of the water.

To stay safe, whirligigs must see in air and in water at the same time. That's why they have split eyes! The top part looks up while the bottom part looks down.

BRIGHT LIGHTS

Would you believe rear ends that glow in the dark? Well, that is the case with fireflies. By day they look like ordinary brown beetles. But at night their flashing lights help them find mates.

Glowworms are wormlike insect grubs with shiny sides. Their saliva hangs down in long, sticky threads. Insects that fly toward the glowworms get stuck in the threads and are soon gobbled up.

?

DID YOU KNOW?

- **Fireflies are not flies. Glowworms are not worms. Both are beetles.**

CRICKETS ON GUARD

In Japan, *tree crickets* sometimes serve as house alarms! They usually chirp all night long. But they stop if someone comes too close! A break in their song signals danger!

The Japanese feed their pet crickets cucumber, lettuce, chestnuts, and beans. Sometimes the owner chews the food first to make it softer. Sick crickets may get mosquito mixed with honey served in special blue and white dishes. That's worth chirping about!

DID YOU KNOW?

- **Tree crickets chirp faster in warm weather and slower when it is cool. They don't have voices, but chirp by rubbing their wings together.**